CREEPY CRAWLIES

Fire Ants

by Kari Schuetz

BLASTOFF! READERS

BELLWETHER MEDIA • MINNEAPOLIS, MN

Note to Librarians, Teachers, and Parents:

Blastoff! Readers are carefully developed by literacy experts and combine standards-based content with developmentally appropriate text.

Level 1 provides the most support through repetition of high-frequency words, light text, predictable sentence patterns, and strong visual support.

Level 2 offers early readers a bit more challenge through varied simple sentences, increased text load, and less repetition of high-frequency words.

Level 3 advances early-fluent readers toward fluency through increased text and concept load, less reliance on visuals, longer sentences, and more literary language.

Level 4 builds reading stamina by providing more text per page, increased use of punctuation, greater variation in sentence patterns, and increasingly challenging vocabulary.

Level 5 encourages children to move from "learning to read" to "reading to learn" by providing even more text, varied writing styles, and less familiar topics.

Whichever book is right for your reader, Blastoff! Readers are the perfect books to build confidence and encourage a love of reading that will last a lifetime!

This edition first published in 2016 by Bellwether Media, Inc.

No part of this publication may be reproduced in whole or in part without written permission of the publisher. For information regarding permission, write to Bellwether Media, Inc., Attention: Permissions Department, 5357 Penn Avenue South, Minneapolis, MN 55419.

Library of Congress Cataloging-in-Publication Data

Schuetz, Kari.
  Fire Ants / by Kari Schuetz.
     pages cm. – (Blastoff! Readers. Creepy Crawlies)
Summary: "Developed by literacy experts for students in kindergarten through grade three, this book introduces fire ants to young readers through leveled text and related photos"– Provided by publisher.
  Audience: Ages 5-8
  Audience: K to grade 3
Includes bibliographical references and index.
  ISBN 978-1-62617-222-7 (hardcover: alk. paper)
  1. Fire ants–Juvenile literature. I. Title.
  QL568.F7.S38 2016
  595.79'6–dc23

                        2015002617

Printed in the United States of America, North Mankato, MN.

Table of Contents

Ants That Attack

Fire ants are **insects** that attack!

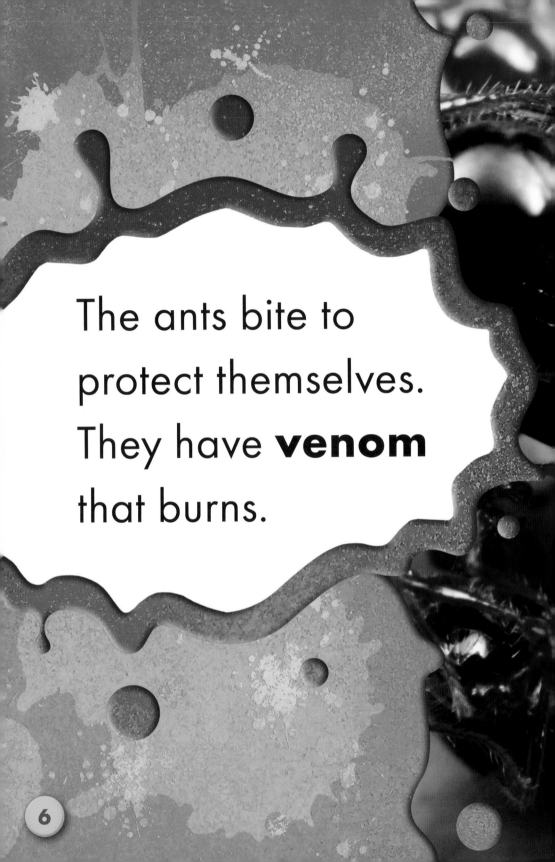

The ants bite to protect themselves. They have **venom** that burns.

The Colony

Fire ants live in **colonies** of up to 500,000 ants.

Most ants in
a colony are
workers. One
queen usually
rules the group.

queen

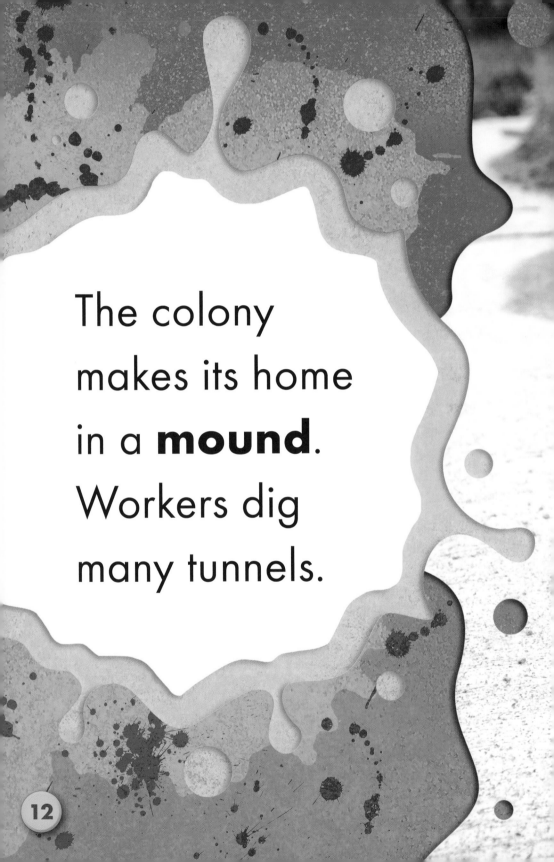

The colony makes its home in a **mound**. Workers dig many tunnels.

mound

Good Workers

Workers leave the mound to **forage**. Some make **scent trails** to food.

Then they bring
caterpillars,
seeds, and other
foods back.

Growing Grubs

This food feeds the queen and her babies. The babies are called **grubs**.

grubs

Grubs need
a lot of care.
But soon they
become workers!

Glossary

colonies—groups of ants that live together

forage—to search for food

grubs—baby ants

insects—small animals with six legs and hard outer bodies; an insect's body is divided into three parts.

mound—a pile of ground where ants live

queen—the ant in a colony that has babies

scent trails—paths marked with a smell

venom—a poison

workers—ants in a colony that find food and do other work

To Learn More

AT THE LIBRARY

Hansen, Grace. *Ants.* Minneapolis, Minn.: Abdo Kids, 2015.

Sayre, April Pulley. *Ant, Ant, Ant!: An Insect Chant.* Minnetonka, Minn.: NorthWord Books for Young Readers, 2005.

Stewart, Melissa. *Ants.* Washington, D.C.: National Geographic, 2010.

ON THE WEB

Learning more about fire ants is as easy as 1, 2, 3.

1. Go to www.factsurfer.com.

2. Enter "fire ants" into the search box.

3. Click the "Surf" button and you will see a list of related web sites.

With factsurfer.com, finding more information is just a click away.

Index

The images in this book are reproduced through the courtesy of: Elliotte Rusty Harold, front cover (large, small); Alex Wild/ Visuals Unlimited/ Corbis, pp. 5, 7, 13; Minden Pictures/ SuperStock, pp. 9, 11; James H. Robinson/ Science Source, p. 15; Deposit Photos/ Glow Images, p. 17; Francesco Tomasinelli/ Science Source, p. 19; Patrick Lynch/ Alamy, p. 21.